NOBODY BUT GOD

TESTIMONIES OF FAITH HOPE AND POWER
DURING THE COVID-19 PANDEMIC

CORINNE SNYDER

Order this book online at www.trafford.com
or email orders@trafford.com

Most Trafford titles are also available at major online book retailers.

Print information available on the last page.

ISBN: 978-1-6987-0515-6 (sc)
ISBN: 978-1-6987-0517-0 (hc)
ISBN: 978-1-6987-0516-3 (e)

Library of Congress Control Number: 2020925437

Cover Design:
Lawrence S Wyche Social Media Manager/Designer

Editors Corinne Snyder, Claudia Brashears, Vermell Byrd McBrayer

KJV
Scripture taken from The Holy Bible, King James Version. Public Domain

NIV
Scripture quotations marked NIV are taken from the Holy Bible, New International
Version®. NIV®. Copyright © 1973, 1978, 1984 by International Bible
Society. Used by permission of Zondervan. All rights reserved. [Biblica]

NLT
Scripture quotations marked NLT are taken from the Holy Bible, New Living
Translation, copyright © 1996, 2004, 2007. Used by permission of Tyndale House
Publishers, Inc. Carol Stream, Illinois 60188. All rights reserved. Website

Trafford rev. 12/23/2020

 www.trafford.com
North America & international
toll-free: 844-688-6899 (USA & Canada)
fax: 812 355 4082

CONTENTS

TESTIMONIES

FAITH

GRATITUDE/THANKFULNESS

HEALING

HOPE

POWER

PROVISION

FOREWORD

HTC Women's COVID -19 Chronicles and Testimonies

We have never seen days like these before where we are navigating times and seasons of epic proportion, previously unimagined. Not only of pandemic and disease but every sector of the earth is affected in an unparalleled manner. Racial and social justice upheavals – rioting and protests – have become all too common. As mounting political unrest and storms abound, the moral fiber of our nation seems to be unraveling. The value and regard of human suffering, for some, seems less important than the value of tangible and perishable commodities and global markets. The earth itself is shaking and shifting, burning and quaking, flooding and melting.

And yet there is a peace that parallels the upheaval. It is like the eye of the storm carefully weaving itself along the uncertain path of the tempest lingering long enough to provide and escape until the next outburst. We are reminded of the Apostle Paul's declaration, *"... we have this treasure in jars of clay to show that this all-surpassing power is from God and not from us. 8 We are hard pressed on every side, but not crushed; perplexed, but not in despair; 9 persecuted, but not abandoned; struck down, but not destroyed."(2 Corinthians 4:7-9,* NIV)Those who are living in the kingdom witness phenomenal break-through, miracle healing, advancement and unexpected record breaking gains in the quality of life. How can it be that during the most catastrophic and chaotic seasons known to man, we are also experiencing astonishing kingdom gains and accomplishments?

The answer is simple, while the earth is cataclysmic and in turmoil, God is not. He remains completely and totally in charge of His people and His earth. *The earth is the Lord's, and the fullness thereof; the world, and they that dwell therein (Psalm 24:1, KJV)*. Although unprecedented, these times and this season, have not suddenly thrust themselves upon us. They have been in the making for a long time. We have heard of them as *'the last days', 'perilous and end times.* They are all part of His master design. Their purpose is to herald a new awakening for kingdom believers, especially in the United States.

And how does the almighty God do that? He reverses the expected outcome by continually showing Himself strong to deliver and mighty to save. He moves in such a fashion that only He can and only He will get the glory. So astonishing are His feats that the Women of Holy Tabernacle Church have taken pause to sit, testify, write and record the remarkable acts of God in their personal lives and in the lives of their families and loved ones.

Hence this book of life-changing and faith building accounts has been chronicled from the women of 'Holy Tab.' These subtle yet mind-blowing, unbelievable yet factual accounts of how a group of ordinary women have endured and emerged as more than conquers in their life's circumstances during the pandemic of 2020 is a compelling must read. Once you pick it up you will not be able to put it down until you have exhausted its contents.

I urge you to read it with an open mind and heart. You'll compassionately identify with the authors and soon their story will become yours. With teary eyes and a kindred spirit they will become your Sistah, mother, auntie and closest friend. You will cry with them, laugh out loud with them and shout victoriously with them as their stories unfold. Your faith will increase as theirs did. You will gain strength to overcome and stand as they did. Courage and boldness will rise up in you to run on and see what the end will be. But I'll let you in on an open secret, in the end we win. A frequent saying of our dearly departed Mother Sarah White reminds us, "We're on the winning side."

I am so joyous and excited, in this season, to be a part of this awe-inspiring and very motivational group of ladies. We are growing closer to one another as our masks and inhibitions are removed. When Missionary Snyder Tabon came up with this novel idea, I was more than willing to support it and her in any way that I could. The more we share and care in transparency, we discover our camaraderie with each other and our bonds are strengthened. We live out and celebrate the fact that God won't put more on you than you can bear and that He makes an escape every time.

Once again, I encourage you to read, savor and enjoy every word of this little book as it will make a great impact on your life. And let us be reminded to live our lives in service to one another with a commitment that, 'If I can help somebody as I travel along then, and only then, my living will not be in vain.'

Respectfully Submitted,
Prophetess Linda Scott
President, Holy Tabernacle Church Women's Ministry

ACKNOWLEDGEMENTS

There are people I like to thank for helping this inspiration from the Lord come to life. I give honor to Bishop Dr. Arthur F. Jack, Pastor of Holy Tabernacle Church, Dorchester, MA. who granted me liberty with this endeavor and to First Lady Angelia Jack for her support. My gratitude to Missionary Delores Quinnerly in whom I consulted with, an author herself, as how to proceed when I was presented with this challenge. I thank God for Prophetess Linda D. Scott, President of the Women's Ministry, for her encouragement in moving this effort forward. I am grateful for the team who encouraged women to write their testimonies and assisted with editing, Minister Vermell Byrd McBrayer and Missionary Claudia Brashears. The group of prayer warriors who consistently put this project before the Lord; praying that God would get the glory and that lives would be changed as a result of this book. Missionaries Gail Appling, Darsalle Boyd, Diane Norman, and Ernestine Wyche, may God continue to bless you. Thank you Missionary Jenita Blair for your assistance in researching various women organizations to which a portion of the proceeds of this book will be donated. To my husband Deacon James Tabon thank you for making it easy for me to work on this venture. Most importantly I want to thank the Women of Holy Tabernacle Church Dorchester, MA. who TOLD THEIR STORIES glorifying and magnifying God. Thank you for allowing us to experience your joy, knowing that God is a very present help in times of need; for NOBODY BUT GOD can do these things.

My Thanks all of you who cheered me along the way.

INTRODUCTION

The year 2020 will not be long forgotten. It was a year in which the whole world was literally brought down to its knees; COVID-19 arrived and a global pandemic took place. The virus dramatically changed our way of life as we knew it. We followed 'stay at home' orders which meant we could only leave our homes when necessary. Some people worked remotely from home, while school children learned their studies remotely from home. Christians were not able to fellowship at Church, so services became virtual. Before the pandemic it was at Church where we worshipped and gave our testimonies about the love and power of God in our lives; and told how God met us in a time of need. We were encouraged and excited about serving God.

The inspiration for this book came as one Saturday I was watching a virtual Women's conference. The Spirit of the Lord impressed upon me that we as women need to tell our stories, and testify of God's goodness, grace and mercy, especially during this time of change and uncertainty. We need to let everyone know that in spite of the pandemic we're living in, God is ever present still transforming the lives and circumstances of His people. Testimonies of faith, hope, and trust demonstrating the power of God during this season should not only be told, but written in a book. I said to the Lord with your help I'm ready for the challenge to assemble these testimonies together.

My own COVID testimony speaks of the comfort and peace that God gave me when my Aunt of 94 years died and went home to be with the Lord. It happened in the early days of the pandemic when rules were rigid, and only a handful of people were allowed to attend her service. But God was faithful for we were still able to celebrate her life in a fitting way and for that I was grateful.

As you read the book, *NOBODY BUT GOD* you will notice how God turned circumstances around from sickness to healing, from being a timid witness to being a bold witness, from an occasional prayer life to an everyday prayer life, from limited finances to expanded finances, or just being thankful in what God had provided for them.

When speaking with the women, who wrote their testimonies, they expressed that their love for God, their prayer life, and reading the word of God increased during this pandemic. Their walk with God became stronger, realizing that God was with them every step of the way. In spite of the obstacles, or weapons formed, they put their trust in God knowing that the weapon formed would not prosper. They wanted to give God the honor and glory due His name; in a time in which many were anxious and fearful, God gave them peace of mind and a grateful heart. They believe that in sharing their testimony, others can know that God will do the same for anyone who puts their faith and trust in Him

Testimonies were placed in categories of: faith, gratitude, healing, hope, power, and provision; you may find some testimonies overlap in more than one category; but no matter what category the testimonies fall into, they showed how God stepped in their lives and changed things around for the good.

I trust that as you read these testimonies you are inspired, and hope that your walk with God is strengthened. My prayer for you is to have a new resolve to serve God, and that you will be a courageous witness telling your story of the goodness, mercy and power of God in your life.

The book was inspired by the following scriptures:

"No weapon that is formed against thee shall prosper; and every tongue that shall rise against thee in judgment thou shalt condemn. This is the heritage of the servants of the LORD, and their righteousness is of me, saith the LORD" *(Isaiah. 54:17,KJV)*.

"Have not I commanded thee? Be strong and of a good courage; be not afraid, neither be thou dismayed: for the LORD thy God is with thee whithersoever thou goest" *(Joshua 1:9,KJV)*.

"Put on the whole armour of God, that ye may be able to stand against the wiles of the devil" *(Ephesians 6:11,KJV)*.

The book was inspired by the following scriptures:

TESTIMONIES

FAITH

FOR WE WALK BY FAITH NOT BY SIGHT

2 CORINTHIANS 5:7

FAITH IN OUR GOD

Giving Honor & Glory to our Lord Jesus Christ. I Thank God for each and every one of you. I pray that as we go through this Season of trials that all has kept the Faith in our God. I have been going through some health issues in that I was in the hospital for three days, which had nothing to do with the Covid19 virus; but I put my trust in God for healing and I came through alright.

Faith to me means trusting and believing in God, as well as applying His word to my life. Romans 10:17,KJV says, "So then faith cometh by hearing, and hearing by the word of God." Also in Ephesians 2:8a, KJV "For by grace are ye saved thru faith and not that of yourselves." My faith was tested while in the hospital and I thank God for His healing power. Once I got home from the hospital I did not go out much, but I encouraged others by praying with them, and letting them know that God has everyone and everything in control. Our faith during this time is being tested as mine was; and in spite of this pandemic, we must always be about our Father's business; for He knows the outcome of all our situations.

So let's keep the faith, keep praying, and reading the Word of God. For He will bring you through no matter what your situation is.

Mother Josephine Shivers

GOD ANSWERS PRAYER

I want to give a testimony to say that God is a healer, in that He healed my daughter and my son-in-law from the Coronavirus. Last month my daughter and son-in-law went to a funeral about 200 miles from where they live. A few days later after they got home my son in law had a fever and had some trouble breathing. A COVID test was done and he came back positive. While trying to take care of her husband my daughter developed a scratchy throat and lost her sense of taste. She was tested and her results came back positive.

I started to pray asking God to heal both of them. I have faith and trust in God because He's never let me down, He always seems to step in and take over when I need Him most. The scripture from Matthew 11:28,KJV kept repeating itself to me, "Come unto me, all ye that labour and are heavy laden, and I will give you rest." This scripture helped to put my mind at ease. I stopped worrying and let God handle this situation, all I could do was to keep praying that God would heal them from the virus. I thank God He healed them from the coronavirus and now they are both back to work. **Prayer Works!**

Judy Blackwell

HE OPENS DOORS

I can truly say God is an amazing God, He has been faithful. I give him all the glory and all the power and all the praise. In March 2020 during the pandemic I was praying and asking the Lord; what can I do during this pandemic to help someone, and make a difference? Lord show me the way I need to go. I thank God he heard my prayers.

One and a half weeks, to be exact, a pastor I had met when I went to Uganda on a mission trip in 2015 called me told me that children are coming to him and saying that he should start a children's home. He said the Lord told him that my husband and I are to be a part of this ministry. So with great prayer and seeking the face of God, He gave me the name Miracle Children's Home. The Pastor told me the children were sleeping on the floor, they didn't have beds to sleep on; and some were even getting sick from sleeping on the floor. That week I used my paycheck to buy some mattresses. The Lord told me you can't keep your mouth shut, you have to open your mouth and ask for help. I was a bit hesitant, but I went to my supervisor at work and ask her if she could join with me to help these children; she gave me $1000. towards the ministry. We bought more mattresses bunk beds, mosquito nets, sheets, and blankets. It was the first time in these children lives that they were able to sleep on a proper bed; they were so excited and so happy.

God has just been blessing this ministry. If you want to do a work for God, just pray and He will open doors for you as He did for me. I thank God for the help of my wonderful husband, co- workers, church family, and others that have been blessing this ministry. I give God thanks, glory and honor, for this ministry. As my Pastor recently preached "Do it quickly, Do it now"; scripture taken from St. John 9:4,KJV "I must work the works of him that sent me while it is day and night cometh, when no man can work," and that is what I'm running with.

Laverne Mejia

MY PSALMS 91 TESTIMONY

Psalm 91:1,KJV says, "He that dwelleth in the secret place of the most High shall abide under the shadow of the Almighty." The entire chapter of Psalm 91 has been my protection and strength during this pandemic. Three times a day I would read that chapter, to get renewed and to build up my faith and trust in God. The 'Stay at Home' order has not been easy for me. Listening to the news all the time about the virus with numbers of people getting sick and with those who died was upsetting to me.

God spoke to me through Psalm 91 and He promised, "There shall no evil befall thee, neither shall any plague come nigh thy dwelling" (Psalm 91:10,KJV). He also promised to, "give his angels charge over thee, to keep thee in all thy ways" (Psalm 91:11,KJV). I believed that God had me covered. Whenever I went out I had to take public transportation. I prayed for traveling mercies, being covered by a shield all around me. Whether it was to go to the grocery store or to the drug store I had to believe that God was with me. As a worker at my Church's food pantry I went every two weeks to help bag and distribute food to those in need. Working with gloves, masks and socially distancing was not always easy. I eventually memorized the entire chapter of Psalm 91, and with the Word of God in my heart I could face the day knowing that God is with me and that I don't have to be fearful of any virus.

Mary Glen

THIS IS ONLY A TEST

While living in a multi-family home during the pandemic, a family member tested positive for the corona virus. During this time all family members in the household were extremely nervous, knowing the uncertainty of the effects the virus would or could have on each family member. Upon speaking with each of our different physicians we were all told, "If a family member was diagnosed positive with the virus, most likely ALL family members will test positive for the virus." Each of our physicians had pre-diagnosed all of us as being positive for the virus, because of our close proximity to each other. I was extremely nervous and on edge as I was awaiting for my COVID test results.

Looking for immediate relief from the worry of the COVID test, the Spirit of God brought to my remembrance a few things. I began to remind myself of a line in the song "You're next in line for a miracle." The particular line in the song says" Have you ever walked the floor?" With that song on my mind, I also remembered part of a prayer my Pastor prayed the last Wednesday before the pandemic, "if anyone of us are afflicted, God will provide healing."

After I was tested the wait of the test results seemed like forever. I prayed for healing, and I trusted God, even though being told in advance by all the Doctors I would more than likely be positive for COVID, due to being in close proximity to the family member who had visible symptoms of COVID and had tested positive. Results were finally provided to me with that of a negative test, despite being in close proximity and sharing common areas with the positive family member. The negative results was against all the Doctors' pre-diagnoses of becoming positive. I knew it was God that protected me from getting the virus. Above all I knew it could only be GOD.

SSB

WHEN YOU PRAY BELIEVE

My testimony is very simple and straight to the point. God is faithful to keep His word. It was my prayer every day for no one in my family to get sick and/or die from this Corona Virus. God honored my prayer and my Dad who is 85 years old, my children, grandson, siblings and their families were all saved from getting the COVID-19 Virus. Not only did He keep them healthy, but kept food on their table, payed for their rent or mortgage, and no one lost their job. Some of my family members were even able to pay off bills and save money.

This pandemic allowed our family to pray more, talk more, love more and take care of each other more. And in spite of this pandemic I thank God that He not only brought us closer to Him, but brought our family closer together to appreciate each other in a greater way. God is certainly true to His word, when you pray in faith believing, He will answer.

"Therefore I say unto you, what things soever ye desire, when ye pray, believe that ye receive them, and ye shall have them" (Mark 11:24,KJV).

Jenita Blair

GRATITUDE/
THANKFULNESS

GIVE THANKS
to the **LORD,**
FOR HE IS GOOD

PSALM 107:1

A TESTIMONY OF GRATITUDE

Take care of God's business and He'll take care of yours. During this time of what others would call uncertainties, I find myself more certain about our God then I've ever been, not because of what He's doing but because of who He is. Think about it. As if His love wasn't enough... He continues to give.

During this Pandemic I have seen God move. We must continue to take God at his word, "Be strong and courageous. Do not be afraid or terrified because of them, for the Lord your God goes with you; He will never leave you nor forsake you" (Deuteronomy 31:6, NIV).

The news focused a lot on essential workers. How many of us after hearing the news felt, "oh well I guess I'm not essential?" Or felt "I will not be able to work" or in my case "I will not be able open my business." I remember thinking, "how would I take care of my customers?" Then God showed up and reminded me who was large and in control, it's God that says who is essential!

Malachi 3:10 it reads "Bring ye all the tithes into the storehouse, and prove me now herewith, if I will not open you the windows of heaven, and pour you out a blessing, that there shall not be room enough to receive it."

I stand here as a witness to all. I wanted to make sure I would be there for my existing customers. God had other plans for the Denard Insurance Agency. We had more NEW policies than we have had in the past 10 years, in other words my business grew during the pandemic. I KID YOU NOT. It just goes to show you can be essential no matter what your position and no matter what your level if you allow God to work through you!

Sister Ida D.

EMMANUEL "GOD IS WITH US"

It is a good thing to have the knowledge of knowing that God is not dead, but He is very much alive. Sometimes when I think of God's goodness, tears form in my eyes, for He has been so good to me. I thank Him for the many years of my life, at 102 years of age.

This has been a strange year for the whole world, life has not been business as usual; as it took a drastic turn for everyone in this year of 2020 due to COVID-19 pandemic. When Churches were told to close its doors and not have any meetings, it became very serious then. We all had to make some changes in our living. We've had to look up to God and trust Him for who He really is: He is supreme, He is Holy, and He is our strong tower. Prayer time, Bible reading in the morning became more and more important. I was more aware of my neighbors, and became more aware of things I could do without.

One day after grocery shopping I put my groceries in the trunk, and then went to another store. I looked for my purse and could not find it. I went back to the grocery store praying and asking God to let me find my purse. My mind was telling me that I was going to find my purse. In it I had a sum of money and cards which I did not want to apply for over again. When I went home I prayed "Father please let someone bring my purse to me. That was Friday evening. The next day, Saturday evening, I got a telephone call asking" did you lose your purse, of course I said yes? The person said I have your purse. O did I ever thank God for that blessing.

That person said she had worked at the post office and it was in the mailbox. She looked in and saw my address and, she said to co-workers I know where she lives, I'll take it to her tonight. She told the night crew, I know that lady we both go to the same Church. So within twenty-four hours God worked the situation out!!. That incident lets me know all the more that God is Emmanuel "God is with us." Praise our God!

Mother Tabitha Goggins

GOD'S ABUNDANT BLESSINGS

Praise God. A new life in Christ Jesus. Thanks be to God for his many blessings. A year that's new to all people in the whole world, with the occurrence of the Corona virus pandemic. But God is merciful, for everyone in my family is well and healthy, no one was sick.

Another of God's abundant blessings, was celebrating my 80th birthday this year. Family from far and near came to help me celebrate: my daughter, sons, grandchildren, friends, sisters and brothers in Christ all came together for the celebration. Cards, phone calls, visits, cakes, flowers, and more which filled me with the great blessings of life. I am grateful to see 80 years of life, but more important to let others know about the grace and mercy of God towards me. He has blessed me abundantly more than I could ever ask or think. Even in this Corona virus pandemic God has been good and has shown His mighty hand in my life.

"I will praise thee; for I am fearfully and wonderfully made: marvelous are thy works; and that my soul knoweth right well" (Psalms 139:14,KJV).

Hallelujah!

Missionary Doris McPherson

GOD'S AMAZING AND AWESOME POWER

My testimony is that God is Awesome. During this time of COVID-19 He's given me new faith and strength in Him every day. I'm reading my Bible more, praying more, and He's teaching me to lean on Him more. Last week I asked God to give me an opportunity to witness to someone, and on the same day God made that happen.

While I was waiting in the checkout line of a department store, there was a young man who asked to go in front of me because he only had a bag of ice, I told him yes he could go in front of me. I had a bible and a devotional for my granddaughter. He saw them and asked if I had little ones. I told him I had a granddaughter who asked for a Bible. At that point I told him I was a Christian who believed in God, and he said he hadn't been to church for a long time. Then the Lord opened up the door for me to witness to him. I just started talking and God did the rest. He told me he wasn't from this area, but was visiting his girlfriend.

I know God is real and true to his word. I know I've gotten closer to God. I thank Him for hearing my prayer and giving me the opportunity to witness to that young man; and I pray that the seed planted will grow so that he comes to know the Lord. I'm trusting God more and more. My faith has increased along with the desire to pray and read his Word. All I can say is that we serve an amazing, loving, caring, and awesome God; in the midst of a pandemic.

Cynthia Israel

IN ALL THINGS GIVE THANKS

During the COVID-19 if it had not been for the Lord on my side I don't know where I would be. My son Earl became sick in September 2019 and was diagnosed with stage four cancer. The doctor said that I should prepare for my son's funeral because he only had another month to live. So I started accompanying my son to the hospital during his chemotherapy sessions bringing prayer and oil every week. September, October, November and December Earl was still living and going to church, Hallelujah! So I asked him if he wanted to get baptized and on January 28, 2020 he was baptized at Church.

When COVID-19 reared its ugly head in March I asked the Lord to keep me from getting exposed to the virus because Earl needed me. God allowed me to continue to go to the hospital with him every week until April. On April 30th he was admitted to the hospital with a fever and they notified me that I could not visit him at this time because of COVID 19. I kept in contact with him on my iPad (Facetime) and was able to encourage him. This was at the same time I was praying for my mom who was sick on a ventilator, two brothers who are fighting cancer, and another brother having complications with diabetes.

I tell you, if it had not been for the Lord on my side I don't know where I would be. The hospital sent my son home on May18th and the next day he passed. I am thankful to God that he gave his life to the Lord and that he was baptized before the pandemic. But in the midst of everything that was going on I heard the voice of the Lord saying to me "in all things give thanks." I know that God will see you through any situation that you're faced with.

Marie Legagneur

LIGHT IN THE DARKNESS

For me it all began with the sudden death of my first born. He was the son that took on the responsibility of caring for his mom, always making sure I had whatever I needed or wanted.

After his death his wife of only three years seemed to have a great resentment towards me. It was like I had somehow taken her husband from her. As I began to let that go and focus on the Lord the Pandemic began to raise its ugly head. Now I am quarantined and really alone. Because I live in a senior complex my family could not visit, and even going to church was not an option; but my church family and my natural family made sure I did not want for anything.

I had way too much time to dwell on my loss. Studying the word of God helped me not to focus on myself. It enabled me to draw closer to God really feeling His presence; which allowed me to accept my son's passing. I am so grateful for the time we had together. Nine Months later I lost my sister who was a year and a half older than I. We were very close as the youngest of my parents 11 children. We did everything together even plan to retire and travel together, but that was not to be.

So within a few months there was the loss of my son, my sister, my dear friend, and another close friend's husband all during this time it was a burden on me. "**But God,**" in the midst of this darkness, there is a welcoming gleam of Light, one of my daughters becomes engaged to be married; and in spite of my afflictions God shows me a glimpse of joy. Surely it is God alone that can give you Joy in the midst of Sorrow. He can lift all your burdens and He can shine light on your path.

As I continue to go through I thank God for allowing me to see His grace and mercy, and I give Him all the Praise.

Karimah Rashid

THANKING GOD FOR COUNTLESS BLESSINGS

I'm so grateful to God for keeping me safe from COVID-19. I have underlining medical conditions that prevents me from going out except for medical appointments. I know that it's the blood of Jesus that covers and protects me when I go out; and I thank God for the health that I have. God has brought me out of many situations. He's has been my Jehovah Jireh, the Lord my provider, each and every day through this pandemic. I miss my Church family and pray for the day that I can return to fellowship with the saints. In the meantime I'm glad for the Zoom meetings, because I can still be in contact with some of the saints.

I am so thankful just to be alive with a burning desire to serve the True and Living God. He is My strength and My sustainer. "God is our refuge and strength, a very present help in trouble" (Psalms 46:1,KJV). May He guide my footsteps so I do not stray.

Freddie Mae Jones

TO GOD BE THE GLORY

My mother and I have been blessed during the pandemic, we are both well (including my mom's caregiver) and we get to spend more time together. Of course I heard about the Covid19 on the news but it really hit me in March when I was on vacation for a couple of days, and when I went back to work I was told that would be the last day in the office until further notice. Then I found out weeks later that someone on the job had contracted Covid19. I thanked God, I did not become infected and brought it home to my mom who is 88 years old and has dementia. My co-worker, thankfully, has recovered. I have been working from home since then, and I thank God I still have a job.

I am a career counsellor that advises mostly the unemployed about resumes, suggesting workshops to attend, and giving information about available jobs. But during this pandemic I have found that a lot of people just needed someone to listen to how scared, frustrated, and uncertain they are about their future. As I listen I hear about bills that can't be paid, children's needs that can't be met, and just being tired of Covid19. I then give suggestions about employment but a lot of times with the guidance of the Holy Spirit I tell them and/or remind them that even with all that's going on God is good and that Prayer changes things. The conversation, most times, then turns out to be more about God's goodness and His grace, than about their situation and it ends with praise, Hallelujah.

As Matthew 18:20,KJV proclaims, "For where two or three are gathered together in my name, there am I in the midst of them." To God Be Glory for the things He has Done, He is Doing and will Do!!

Claudia Brashears

HEALING

HE IS MY

Healer

EXODUS 15:26

BUT GOD

Just before the 'stay at home' order was announced due to the coronavirus pandemic, I had major surgery on my thyroid gland. After 15 years of ill health, hospital visits, and diagnostic tests a tumor was found on my thyroid that was the cause of my health issues, and surgery was performed. It was nothing but the grace of God that was keeping me alive.

Doctors told me that this was a very complex situation, because the tumor was next to the vocal cords, and I could be worse off if surgery was performed to take the tumor out. All I kept hearing doctors say was 'she will not be able to speak or sing.' Singing is something I love to do.

I prayed and I fasted before the Lord about the situation. I tell you nobody but God stepped in. Because of my complex case I was evaluated by a world renown specialty doctor who performed vocal cord surgery on celebrity singers. He gave it to me straight and said this surgery cannot wait and he could not promise that I would have my vocal cords and nerves intact based on the test results. I looked him straight in his face and said I know a man name Jesus, He will take care of me!

Well God showed up and showed out! The doctor was amazed and shocked at what happened. During the surgery they found the tumor was almost the size of a grapefruit and that it just slid out without touching vocal cords or having doctors to shave vocal cords or nerves.

No damage to nerves or vocal cords, and no cancer Hallelujah!!! I can speak and I can sing!!! Know that there's nothing God can't do. Just put your trust in Him, because we are in his hands! **Hallelujah!**

Missionary Darsalle Boyd

GOD IS STILL BLESSING, IN THE MIDST OF A PANDEMIC

On March 11, 2020 my husband was getting ready for work around 6a.m. When he cried out to me, I can't feel my legs!!!!I sat up in bed and said let me get the Joint Flex pain relief cream. I was thinking maybe you're just having legs cramps. I was still sleepy from working late the night before. As I was getting out of bed, I realize my husband was having a stroke. My husband's face was twisted up on his right side of his body. I was kind of thrown off because I was telling myself, my husband is only 42 years old. I can't be a widow at 42.

God What Is This? My husband started to cry and kept saying I can't feel my legs. I told my husband we have to call 911. My husband said, please don't call 911 just drive me to the hospital. I was thinking in my head how am I going to get you to the hospital if you can't walk. I said to my husband let's pray, because you can't walk and I don't know how I was going to get my husband to the car.

We started to pray and ask God to HELP us get to the hospital. I grab the bottle of oil my pastor had given me, and put some on my husband and myself. My husband was able to crawl down the steps to get to the car. By the Grace of God, we were able to get him to the hospital.

The doctor said he was lucky to get to the hospital in time because he had a small blockage in his brain, which had cause him to have a stroke and his blood pressure was very high. I would not call it lucky I call it God's Grace and Mercy that kept my husband alive.

"So, my dear brothers and sisters, be strong and immovable. Always work enthusiastically for the Lord, for you know that nothing you do for the Lord is ever useless"

(1 Cor.15:58, NLT).

We Thank God for Keeping Us, Safe in the Midst of a Pandemic. God is Still Blessing, In the Midst of a Pandemic.

Shirby Lilley

HE MADE ME WHOLE

By the beginning of June the pandemic was raging. As usual on mornings I get up and pray thanking God that He kept me through the night. I gave God the glory and the praise for another day. On this particular morning after I got up and I felt a pain on my side. As I continued to make my bed, the pain got worse and worse. I began to pray even more and asked God to touch my body. As I prayed the pain wasn't letting up at all. I was feeling even worse. The more I prayed the worse it got, but I had to go to the hairdresser, so I continued to get ready. I just kept praying asking the Lord to touch my body.

I made it to the hairdresser, and I kept praying and asking God to touch my body, I kept saying "I know you're able God"; and I know you can heal me again. Nobody in the shop knew I was in any pain. I just kept praying and trusting God. I was thinking that God would have at least relieve me just a little bit, but the pain remained. By the time I left the hairdresser I was in so much pain I barely made it to the car. I made it home and it was all I could do to get in the house and lay down on the couch. I told my husband to call our granddaughter and tell her to come over. I did not want to go to the hospital because of the pandemic, but my children made me call the hospital and they told me to come right in.

By the time I got to the hospital the pain had subsided. Doctors ran all types of tests, and at that time they believed it might have been a problem with my gallbladder. Results of all tests came back negative. I thank God for His healing and His delivering. Through it all I was trusting God. Final determination of the doctors was they found nothing wrong.

I continue to give God the praise because He is a Healer. Healing means to make whole, and to this day I still have no pain. "O LORD my God, I cried unto thee, and thou hast healed me" (Psalms 30:2,KJV).

Reverend Fredda Simpson

LOOK WHAT THE LORD HAS DONE!

Back in the latter part of 2019, I was faced with a health challenge. On December 24th I had surgery. After being in surgery for 4 hours, I am told, the doctors came out to my family and gave a report. The surgery took 7 ½ hours. While riding through the storm, walking through the valley of shadow of death I thank God He was with me. God's hands was upon me, during the surgery. And while still in recovery, I've had to stand on my Faith in God, declaring and decreeing the Word of God; binding and loosing in the name of Jesus.

"I shall not die, but live, and declare the works of the LORD" (Psalms118:17,KJV). "and with his stripes we are healed" (Isaiah 53:5c, KJV). I am healed by the stripes of Jesus. "He took up our infirmities and bore our diseases" (Matthew 8:17b, NIV). Jesus carried my infirmity and my sickness

"For I will restore health unto thee, and I will heal thee of thy wounds, saith the LORD;"

(Jeremiah 30:17a, bKJV).

I break, rebuke, and cast out any spirit that attempts to establish itself to my body. I speak life, healing and strength over my body; knowing that my "beauty shall be as the olive tree," (Hosea14:6b, KJV).

Then came COVID-19.

While spending time with the Lord in my kitchen on August 1, 2020 praying, thanking Him I had an epiphany!

C-Charlene's
O-Omnipotent
V- Virtual
I - Intentional
D- Deliverance From the hand of the enemy.
19-The number 19 in numerology represents the beginning or closing of a season of time. According to the Bible, number 19 is used as a symbol of faith.

He (God) shut the Whole World Down just for my Healing because I AM the Apple of His Eye! Hallelujah! Thank you, Jesus! I'm Grateful! Hold my Mule!

In Jesus Name,
Charlene Phillips

THROUGH THESE EYES I SEE THE GLORY

Earlier this year I was having issues with my eyes. I was having difficulty seeing even when wearing my glasses. I decided to go and see the eye doctor. I was thinking I needed to change my glasses, but to my surprise the doctor informed me, I had cataracts and in both eyes. I really didn't know how to feel or what to think. I was more in shock because I really thought I was going to upgrade my eye glass prescription.

After the news sunk in, I discussed my options with my husband. We knew this was serious and didn't want to waste time. We decided surgery was the best option. I made the appointment, but shortly after it was made COVID happened and my surgery was put off for months.

While I was home in quarantine I prayed and ask God to take me through this rough time, and to be with me during the eye surgery having no complications. I was nervous about having eye surgery, but I know God was with me. He gave me two scriptures to meditate on, "I will lift up mine eyes unto the hills, from whence cometh my help; my help cometh from the LORD, which made heaven and earth" (Palms 121:1,2,KJV); as well as Psalms 50:15,KVJ "And call upon me in the day of trouble: I will deliver thee, and thou shalt glorify me."

I was finally able to have my surgery in September, and praise God HE brought me through. I am able to see so much better now, not only naturally, but spiritually. Spending more time with God during this time has also opened my spiritual eyes. All we have to do is to call on the Lord God and pray, our help only comes from God. I still have one more eye surgery to go, and I will continue to trust God as He was with me for the first eye, He'll be with me for the second eye.

In Jesus name Amen.

Delores Brown

HOPE

FOR WITH

God

NOTHING

SHALL BE

impossible

LUKE 1:37

BE A GOOD WITNESS

First I want to thank God for who He is ; the head of my life and the Author and Finisher of my Faith. He is Sovereign, My Savior, My beginning, My end, My all in all. I want to thank Him for his keeping power and His Saving Grace Which is New Every Day. So grateful to be in the will of God at a time such as this.

This Corona virus is a serious matter to hear and witness so many people passing away. Every day that the Lord has kept me and my love ones it's a blessing. He continues to Supply All our needs according to His purpose. My husband, son and daughter are still employed where so many lost their jobs, I thank the Lord for Divine Favor.

Last week I was out shopping and a young man was selling items from his truck. He introduced me to some masks 50 in a box for $10.00. I thought it was a great deal, the good masks the surgical ones, I brought them and he gave me the masks with $10.00 back in change. I proceeded to walk away and continued to shop at another store. I then realized I never went into my pocket book to pay the man for the masks. I went back to explain that he gave me $10.00 that did not belong to me. He assumed he was giving me change for there was a number of people he was dealing with at the same time.

A couple of people were standing there listening to what was taking place. The young man expressed his gratitude saying "God is good," the reaction from others YES HE IS. My response was "there are still good people in the world." He thanked me for being honest, and I said "it was the right thing to do".

I always want to be a witness of God's goodness and grace to others. I just wanted to share the Love, Joy, and Hope of God. "For I am persuaded, that neither death, nor life, nor angels, nor principalities, nor powers, nor things present, nor things to come, Nor height, nor depth, nor any other creature, shall be able to separate us from the love of God, which is in Christ Jesus our Lord" (Rom.8:38-39,KJV).

Evangelist Laverne Johnson

GOD DID NOT BRING ME THIS FAR TO LEAVE ME

2020 has been a challenging year, but also one that has opened many eyes. God has kept me. He was a friend and companion. He has been a provider, by touching my employers so that I could work full time at home and get paid my regular salary when others got laid off or got a cut in salary. Many of the staff laid off were rehired when we reopened. God kept me alive and healthy. He kept a roof over my head and all my bills paid.

I gained a whole new appreciation for freedoms I took for granted. It was a great time of reflection for me and putting life into perspective. I really leaned on God for strength and peace of mind even when those around me seemed full of panic and fear. I appreciate my church family, my biological family, friends and co-workers so much more and how much they mean to me.

I can't wait till things are truly back to normal, or as close to normal as possible, and even better because I believe there has been an awakening within myself and the world from this pandemic.

The scripture which says it all for me is found in Philippians "I can do all things through Christ which strengtheneth me" (Philippians 4:13,KJV).

God bless you.

Missionary Christina Williams

GOD'S GOT IT UNDER CONTROL

Before the Coronavirus pandemic I was worried about getting a job to the point I was upset all the time and crying. Then when the pandemic started and was on quarantine, I cried out to God what am I going to do? God told me to be patient, and be still, relax and not to worry, about getting a job. Just concentrate on Me. Stay calm, I got it under control. You know Me, just put your trust in Me. It was a release for me. I stopped worrying about getting a job and focused on staying in the house and being safe.

There are women who live in my building that have disabilities, and they were also nervous and aggravated about not going to work. It was hard for them to understand why they had to stay home and not go to work. When I saw how upset and nervous they were I thanked God for what He did for me, telling me to stay calm and be patient. I told them what God had told me, not to worry and relax, because I was nervous too about things and now I'm a lot calmer. I told them that God is in this with us and no matter what, God has us, and we're going to be OK.

Kevena Fauvre

GOD'S HEALING GRACE

During the COVID-19 pandemic I experienced many situations in which God stepped in; however I can only tell one. I faced a couple of physical challenges, but God let me know that His promises are sure and that HE is with me.

First of all I have vertigo with dizzy spells occurring three and four times a day; wondering why it has all of a sudden resurfaced and so fiercely. Living alone with dizziness can be frightening; and second of all I have respiratory problems in which it's difficult for me to breathe at times. My carpet has to be removed in order to make it easier for me to breathe.

I refuse to allow this virus to keep me from living my life that God, not the virus, gave me. In spite of all this, I believe that God will not have me to suffer with extreme dizziness and not being able to breathe.

Jeremiah 29:11,NIV says, "I know the plans I think towards you declares the Lord. Plans to prosper you and not harm you, plans to give you hope and a future." So because God is faithful to His promises, He promised me hope and a future. I have found comfort because in the word, God said I will not leave you alone. So, knowing that I am never alone, I will not worry about my physical challenges, for God has given me peaceful rest.

Phyllis Dunn

GOD IS OUR PRESENT HELP

Part of my formula for 'survival' during the pandemic is remaining prayerful, continuing to trust in God for my well-being. The pandemic has allowed me to be in more communication with God foremost, knowing He is right beside me. My family and friends near and far that have been too busy to meet and share in conversation prior to the pandemic are closer now than before. We've shared about plans and occasions to look forward to as a family and for that I am grateful.

I Praise the Lord He's blessed me, and spared my life to see another birthday during this time, and that my children were able to travel and celebrate it with me. God continues to keep me as I pay more attention to my health, while amending some of my habits. I certainly have missed going to the physical church being able to fellowship with the saints, but I have been in telephone contact with them, which makes me feel that I'm still in touch with the saints.

We may not know how long we will be in this period of uncertainty and doubt, but we know that, "God is our refuge and strength, a very present help in trouble" (Psalm46:1,KJV).

I trust Him and believe that God will bring us through.

Mother Gloria Jefferson

GOD IS WITH US THROUGH OUR STORMS

Being faced with medical issues all my life, the challenges of those issues worsened during this COVID -19 Pandemic. Just before the Pandemic my transplanted kidney developed cancer, and therefore stopped working. Cancer was also found in one of my lungs. I had a combination of chemotherapy and radiation treatments for a few weeks.

All during the quarantine when people were on lock down, I had to travel to the hospital at least three times a week for cancer therapy and for dialysis. I was physically and mentally tired. I was asked questions by doctors and I told them to write Do Not Resuscitate orders on my records. I told them just let me go, don't try to bring me back. I know where I'm going; I'll be in the arms of Jesus. I was praying for some relief from my situation. I just continued praying to God to help me through this situation. He has always helped me; for He's never failed me yet.

I then found myself encouraging someone else who was on dialysis like myself. I was telling them how my faith is in Christ Jesus, and even though I'm in the situation that I'm in God is with me, and if this is my time to go God is still with me. I started to think about my children and how I still need to be here to encourage them to seek God first for everything; so I can't go anywhere yet!

But in spite of my all my medical conditions, I would never give up Jesus. He has been with me my whole life. I thank God the latest x-ray showed that I'm cancer free. I know God is with me even in the midst of this pandemic.

Maxine Scott

I MAY NOT UNDERSTAND
BUT I TRUST GOD

"Trust in the Lord with all thine heart; and lean not unto thine own understanding. In all thy ways acknowledge him, and he shall direct thy paths" (Proverbs 3:5,6,KJV).

What do you do when it seems like everything you worked so hard for seems to change or erupt right before your eyes. Imagine one person makes a decision to change their life and that decision disrupts your life. After working at the same job for 20 years my employer told me the business would be closing. I was blind-sided! My life was comfortable. I was able to take care of things I needed and things I enjoyed. I really did not see it coming!

What do you do when you don't know what to do? You pray and trust in the Lord. I began to spend time with the Lord, because I knew He was the one who had all the answers. He allowed me to find another job; it was not like what I had previously, but I was grateful. Things were getting better. Then a couple of months later the COVID-19 Pandemic happened. The state of affairs with the pandemic was enough to deal with, but then I found myself in an even harsher situation. I had been living in my residence for over eighteen years and now during this pandemic my landlord tells me she is not renewing my lease, and I must move. When I asked her why she says nothing you've done. Her words were "I just need the Apartment."

I began to cry out to the Lord asking him "why is this happening?" Things seem to really be getting hard for me. At this point I am mentally, physically and emotionally drained.

God kept giving me the scripture from Proverbs 3:5,6 to rely on. "Trust Me," God said, don't depend on man; I will guide you. I have been practicing patience and trust in God. I'm living with family temporarily, and I know God has something better for me.

I can truly say that I thank God for being in my life, it makes me wonder what would happen If I did not know Christ. But I do know Him, and He promised He would never leave me nor forsake me, I will continue to put my trust in Him.

Vanyetta Thomas

NEVER GIVE UP

Living through the COVID-19 Pandemic continues to prove to me that God is real. All of my life God has shown up when I needed Him most; when I needed healing, when I needed a place to stay, and when I needed a friend. So living during this COVID-19 time is no different with what God can do. I am older now and live alone yet God continues to be with me. I am not afraid or worried, because Jesus said He would be with me until the end and I Praise God for that. He has been so good to me!!

During this time I have been protected when traveling to and from the grocery store or the drug store. God gave me wisdom in how to speak with management concerning an incident that happened at a drug store. I received poor customer service from an employee who was rude on more than one occasion and had placed misinformation into my records.

The Holy Spirit has a way of calming us and helping us to refocus when we want to go off course. Thank you Jesus for being so good to me, I know that you will bring me out of this pandemic situation just as you have brought me out of other situations in the past.

"O Lord, thou art my God; I will exalt thee, I will praise thy name; for thou hast done wonderful things; thy counsels of old are faithfulness and truth" (Isaiah 25:1,KJV).

Margaret Mc Daniel

PUT ALL YOUR CARES ON HIM

Living during this time of the Coronavirus has allowed me to have a closer walk with God. Some of the benefits of this walk have been: more praying and more reading the Word of God. I thank God, as people in my company was being laid off, my job was intact. God protected me from the virus, as my job requires going into the homes of many people. I was nervous about the virus and nervous about sharing how God helped me; but then realized I had to trust that God would protect me and I had to share with people letting them know that God is still blessing even while we're in this pandemic.

So I started encouraging family members, my consumers (people who I work with in their homes) and others that God can do all things. I would share the scripture God gave me, "Casting all your care upon him; for he careth for you" (I Peter 5:7,KJV). Once I started to take more time with God I started to trust Him more putting everything in His hands. He took the fear away of being able to talk to people about God during this pandemic. I had opportunities to share with my consumers, which are about 100 people, as well as my family about the love of God in the midst of a pandemic.

When you put all your anxieties, all your problems and all your worries on Jesus, He will take care of you and see you through.

Kadenya Campbell

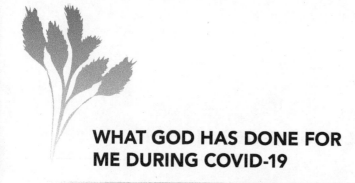

WHAT GOD HAS DONE FOR ME DURING COVID-19

During the pandemic, God taught me how to be an effective Prayer Warrior. He taught me that prayer wasn't just about me but that it was about me knowing how to intercede for others; our children, grandchildren, Mothers, Fathers, Churches, the sick-shut in and more. He taught me to pray without ceasing; staying on the line with Jesus Christ continually. Because I have been praying more, my love for God has grown. I love Him more and more each day.

When someone ask me to pray for them or for their family, I don't wait, I pray right then. I thank God every day, for I know with assurance that prayer is the key to all situations in life. He'll hear EVERY WORD you say and ANSWER all your prayers. I know that prayer changes people and situations. There is a prayer always in my heart going up to my Lord and Savior.

I love to pray to God especially during this Pandemic, because this is what it's going to take to heal our land. "Pray one for another, that ye may be healed. The effectual fervent prayer of a righteous man availeth much" (James 5:16b, c, KJV).

Sherain Moseley

POWER

No, in all these things we are more than conquerors *through* HIM *who* loved *us.*

ROMANS 8:37

"COVID-19 EXPERIENCE"

During this pandemic God has allowed me to go into work daily. I set my vacation time at the beginning of the year so, when my Church has Holy Convocation, a week of nightly Worship services, I will have the time off. Well, due to Covid-19 everything was shut down, including churches. But my vacation was still on and I planned to do a 'stay-cation.'

On the third day of my 'stay-cation' I woke up in excruciating pain; my lower back, left hip and both knees. I took medication to ease the pain, but it was not working, it just helped me sleep a little. My week vacation had come to an end, but the pain had not. I called my job to say that I would not be in on Monday morning.

As I laid on my bed I had a vision and sensed two people discussing my condition with the focus on the medication I was taking. After another night of; O God, help me Jesus, please come see about me, I called the job to say that I was still in pain, and asked for the rest of the week off. I found myself walking even worse than before. I went to my doctor and she ordered; blood work, prescription for pain and an X-Ray. I took the medication, but it was not giving me the result I needed.

I remembered and began to sing songs that my mother use to sing. "Lord I need you to touch me, touch me with your power divine." "Reach out and touch the Lord as he passes by, you'll find he's not too busy to hear your heart's cry." The Spirit of God moved, as I sang and prayed. I began to feel the pain easing up. When I went back to the doctor, I told her I felt better.

Prayer and the Word of God was the answer all along. God restored my strength, just as He said He would. In the midst of this pandemic, I cried unto the Lord and He heard me and delivered me out of all my fears. No matter what the day brings, He has assured me that He is with me.

Josie Spivey

DIVINE PROTECTION

It was Saturday, March 14th at our Missionary meeting that we discussed COVID 19 and what impact it was having globally. Our Missionary President encouraged us to stay vigilant in prayer and be strong in the Lord. She presented us with a flyer with an acronym for COVID 19. The words for COVID 19 read CHRIST OVER VIRUSES AND INFECTIOUS DISEASES the scripture verse relating to 19 is Joshua 1:9,NIV "Have I not commanded you? Be strong and courageous. Do not be frightened and do not be dismayed for the Lord your God is with you wherever you go." This scripture resonated in my heart and I immediately received it in my spirit. I felt God was speaking directly to me.

As the days went by and changes related to COVID were occurring rapidly, I started to develop some anxiety about my safety. I even dreamed that I caught the virus. I rebuked that dream and began to speak life over myself and my situation. I asked God for His divine protection over my health and life. I pleaded the blood of Jesus against any "weapon being formed against me shall not prosper, (Isaiah 54:17a, KJV). I declared God's word in Luke 10:19,KJV that, 'God has given me power to tread upon serpents and scorpions and over all the power of the enemy and nothing shall by any means hurt me.' Praying and declaring his word gave me the strength and power every day to do whatever I needed (work, shop, and take care of family members) without fear and anxiety.

Even during the height of the outbreak when two of my co-workers who I sit very close to came down with the virus; I knew that God was answering my prayer. "God is my refuge and strength" (Psalms 46:1a, KJV). He was my protection then and is still my protection now.

Other scripture verses prayed were: Psalms 91:1, "He that dwelleth in the secret place of the most High shall abide under the shadow of the Almighty," and Psalms 91:10, KJV, "There shall no evil befall thee, neither shall any plague come nigh thy dwelling." No matter what comes my way during this pandemic and for the rest of my life; I trust and believe that God will always be with me.

Missionary Gail Appling

FROM UNEQUIPPED TO EQUIPPED

Little did I know in March 2020 I would be sent home from work because of a pandemic, and was told I would need to work from home. I was asked if I had a computer and I said yes.

What I didn't have was internet, I had no need for it. I didn't even have cable. If I needed internet I would use my phone. So for the first couple weeks I used my phone with the hotspot and I eventually ran out of data. I had to buy cable with internet.

Once I had cable with internet, my employer redeployed me to a job in which I had no instruction or the proper tools to do the job. The reassignment of the job really got to me. I couldn't eat, I couldn't sleep, and I was nervous all the time.

So I started to pray and I ask God to help me. I can't remember all that I said but all I know is nobody but God. He is the only one that can calm your fears. Within the next couple of days I was redeployed back to the job I had been doing for 15 years.

Thank you Jesus! Hallelujah! Nobody but God.!

I might have been unequipped as far as having internet for my job, but I was equipped with the power of God within me to pray and change that job situation.

Ephesians 6:11,KJV says, "Put on the whole armour of God, that ye may be able to stand against the wiles of the devil."

Sandra Carswell

GOD DID NOT FAIL ME

About mid-March my son started to complain of how tired he was. He slept for about two days and he was still tired. Then he lost the taste in his mouth so I checked his temperature and it was elevated. I prayed and anointed him and encouraged him to get tested for COVID-19, he did and the results were positive.

Later on he started to have dizzy spells, fainting, falling and my daughter ordered me to get out of the house. I remember praying "I will not fear." As Psalm 91: 5 -6,KJV says, "Thou shalt not be afraid of the terror by night, nor for the arrows that flies by day, nor for the pestilence that walketh in darkness, nor for the destruction that wasteth at noon day." God is faithful, He did not fail me. His word was my strength and I was determined not to lose my son.

I left the house, called my friends and triggered a prayer connection. GOD came through big time. About four weeks later, my son began to feel better with the help of his children who also were tested, with negative results. Then about two weeks after that he got up and could take care of himself. Now my son is fine and back to work.

PRAISE THE LORD.

Missionary Patricia Jackson

GOD IS MY SHIELD & DEFENCE!!

As a healthcare provider working in a private care facility, I was assigned to the COVID Unit. During my tenure at the unit, it was very nerve wrenching seeing so many deaths around me. At the time when I was assigned to the unit, 29 patients were infected with the virus and within 8 days 19 of those patients died. I've seen death before, but nothing like this.

It was very difficult working in these conditions especially when the family of the patients were not allowed to visit; from my vantage point it was unbearably sad because they died alone, and that bothered me very much! At one point, a new patient was brought in and the staff was warned to apply extra precaution because the patient was highly contagious. With that being said no one wanted to expose themselves to this new patient. Eventually, I volunteered because she was too weak from the virus to help herself. While I was assisting her my face mask broke, I had to run quickly to the bathroom to take off my face shield, re-sterilize it, and then replace the broken mask.

I have to give GOD all the praise for His protection, His covering, and His guidance because death was all around; unfortunately, some of my co-workers became infected with the virus. The Holy Spirit had instructed me that it was time to leave this unit, so I requested a transfer, and it was granted to me immediately. "Thank you Lord for allowing me to walk away virus free"!

Looking back in retrospect it brings tears to my eyes seeing how much GOD loves me, knowing that His Angels were encamped around me! The scripture that was embedded in my spirit throughout this experience was Psalm 23:4a, KJV GOD You really took me "through the valley of the shadow of death."

"GOD YOU ARE A GOOD, GOOD FATHER, THANK YOU LORD!"

Denise Morgan

HE WILL GIVE YOU PEACE IN
THE MIDST OF YOUR STORM

Jesus has 'showed up' during this pandemic. It's not the time to stop and ponder or wonder if this is God's doing or not. But to trust Him while in the storm. As an educator of students of special education, who have an Individual Education Plans, we have to keep a paper trail of any type of incident that takes place. One particular young man had a large folder, to the point that our particular school was not the right place for him.

It was two weeks before the school shut-down, I had to meet with his mom, whom I've known for over 8 years. I had the privilege of teaching both of her other kids' four years each. The 'parent advocate' and headmaster would be present for this meeting. I had heard the comments that other teachers shared that took place from their meeting with her. Knowing a day before the meeting, I got a chance to have a little talk with Jesus.

For 30 minutes or more, during the meeting, I had to endure her verbal abuse. I could not believe what was coming out of her mouth. She was so obnoxious' I was called everything' but a child of God. Yelling 'I don't like her son' I'm lying on him' he said he did not do any of those things, I believe my child, and my child doesn't lie. Although I wasn't able to calm her down, I was calm. Hallelujah, God showed up within me!

Two months into the online zoom learning, mom saw what we all had been trying to say. God is still showing us to not give up, trust Him during this time. People are dying all over this world. Prayers are going up. Riots and killings are going on, but He showed me even with this He is still with us in the storm. "Be of good cheer; I have overcome the world" (John 16: 33b, KJV).

Missionary Ernestine Wyche

"I WILL FEAR NO EVIL: FOR THOU ART WITH ME"

"Yea, though I walk through the valley of the shadow of death, I will fear no evil: for thou art with me: thy rod and thy staff they comfort me ... thou anointest my head with oil; my cup runneth over" (Psalms 23:4,5b, c, KJV).

During this pandemic God gave me a powerful "AH HA" moment regarding these words. This moment did not come while I was on my knees praying or while I was in church worshipping. This moment came while I was standing in the social distancing line at a supermarket waiting for my turn to go in and pick up a few items.

I was looking around at the people waiting to go in and those leaving the store. Then all of a sudden, it was as if a tidal wave hit me and these words swept over me, "I will fear no evil: for thou art with me". Having a personal relationship with the Heavenly Father makes all the difference in the world when there is sickness and diseases all around you.

Those words swept over me so forcefully that I felt as if a ton of bricks lifted from my shoulders. I realized that God had just given me a reality check. At this moment, I realized that I was experiencing an – "AH HA SO THIS IS WHAT THIS SCRIPTURE REALLY MEANS MOMENT!"

Those words just kept echoing in my mind and the tears began welling up in my eyes. It seemed as though every step that I took, the words began getting louder and more real to me. The thought that my Father was with me with every step that I was taking had become so overwhelming to me.

The excitement for me was the reality of knowing that I had nothing to fear because God was right there with me. I felt as if I was floating. The Lord had anointed my head with the oil of joy and peace; and my cup was running over.

At this moment, God was letting me know that the corona virus truly was no match for His power and protection.

Minister Vermell Byrd McBrayer

THE POWER OF GOD

I thank God for His power through this time of COVID.-19. I had to pray and pray for myself, as well as for others. It got hard sometimes, because I had episodes of dizziness and became weak; but I had to press on to God and hold on to Him.

Some days I cried, but I was still holding on to God's unchanging hand. Every time I had a spell of dizziness and got weak God brought me back, after praying with the power of God that's within me. I truly thank God for this time, for I was able to examine myself and get closer to God. This time has allowed my faith and my prayer life to get stronger. I know that without Him I cannot make it. It's His power that keeps me, and it's His power that sustains me.

"Trust in the LORD with all thine heart; and lean not unto thine own understanding. In all thy ways acknowledge him, and he shall direct thy paths." (Proverbs 3:5-6,KJV)

Remember to always trust God.

Missionary Dorothy Hurd

THE WONDERFUL WORKS OF GOD

About 6 months before the pandemic came to the United States, God gave me some instructions to do something I thought was strange, but I didn't question God. Every morning I did what God commanded me to do.

All of a sudden this pandemic broke out, and my job sent me to some of the most dangerous cities and towns; where the COVID virus rate was high. I was treated badly by some people; but in spite of it all, God's protection kept me mentally, emotionally, and physically, during that time.

My job now has weekly testing for the Corona virus which was one of my answered prayers. I realized that the seemly strange instructions God gave me before the pandemic was actually to prepare me for this time. God is faithful to His people. Proverbs 3:5,KJV scripture says, "Trust in the LORD with all thine heart; and lean not unto thine own understanding."

Tonya Ward

PROVISION

Trust *in the* LORD *with all your* Heart.

PROVERBS 3:5

"ALL THINGS WORK TOGETHER FOR THE GOOD"!

I had two unplanned minor procedures that were very expensive at the end of 2019 leading into 2020. I did not have the money outright, so I opted to put the expenses on my credit card and planned to teach over the February Break (like I do every year) in order to help pay the balance. For some reason, this year they rejected my application for the job. I was upset with the news because rejection is never a good feeling and also I was concerned about how I would get out of the financial hole I was in.

My family and work commitments make it difficult for me to find opportunities to get extra income so I prayed that God would show me what to do. Well, fast forward a few months later-COVID hit. I was forced to stay home and everything I thought I had planned (dinners with friends, travel plans, weddings, elevation conference etc.) was canceled.

The bible says, "We know that in all things God works for the good of those who love Him, who have been called according to His purpose"(Rom. 8:28, NIV). I believe that in the midst of everything that was going on, God worked out this situation for my good. Staying home for all of these months changed my spending habits to be mostly on groceries. So, being forced to be locked down, put me in a position where I was able to pay off debt from those procedures and to begin saving more money. I guess I did not need that teaching job over the February break after all! God said no for a reason.

I have also loved the way that God has allowed me to be able to spend more time with my family and more time with Him! The multifaceted impacts of COVID certainly have been challenging for me, but I know that God is a God of promises and that He will do just what he says! He has divinely connected me with women that have helped support my mental, emotional, and spiritual growth during such a challenging time and for that, I am forever grateful!
Blessings

Danielle Blair

GIVE WITH A WILLING HEART

God is above all gods and all things, I love Him! Nobody can come between me and My God. I love my God, all thanks and praise go to Him. The COVID Pandemic was a time in which God made a way out of no way for me.

I was laid off from my job with no income coming in. When I received my tax returns the Lord laid specific people on my heart to bless financially in my family and specific friends. One family member was hard to get in contact with. I persisted until I got in touch with him. He was so appreciative because he was not working and had no income.

Meanwhile I am still out of work, and not known to me God was putting His provision in place for me. I had met a couple a few months earlier through my former Employer; who said they would need someone to care for their son while in the hospital giving birth to their second child. The time came for the birth and they called me. I lived in their house to care for their son for 2-3 days. When they paid me I was absolutely amazed. God had multiplied. What they paid me was twice as much as what I received from my tax returns. Hallelujah!

I learned whatever you have don't hold back, give with a generous heart! If God tells you to give, we should give with a cheerful heart. I had no idea that God would bless me in that way. I was reminded of the scripture "Give, and it shall be given unto you; good measure, pressed down, and shaken together, and running over, shall men give into your bosom. For with the same measure that ye mete withal it shall be measured to you again" (Luke 6:38,KJV).

I praise God for He does all things well, no matter what it looks like, even in the midst of a pandemic.

Brenda Kirwan

GOD'S PROVISION

I wanted to take a moment to share my testimony because I can't stress enough how good God has been to me. Right before quarantine I was laid off from work with no pay and had just gotten diagnosed with a heart condition. I had been working for this same company for almost a year, and had been dealing with health issues, however losing my job was tough. I felt as if I had to choose between taking care of myself and going to work. I rely solely on my own income to provide for myself, and getting laid off put me in a vulnerable position.

Here I was, with no job, in physical pain, and suffering from Post-traumatic stress disorder due to an unhealthy relationship I had just ended. I had no other option but to trust God. I know God has been good to me, He has shown Himself Almighty.

During quarantine I never starved. The fainting stopped and the pain has decreased dramatically. The nightmares I had subsided. Not one utility has been turned off and I still have a roof over my head. I am at peace, but most importantly I have experienced the greatest source of joy that compares to no other, the joy that only God can give.

I may not be fully well, or have a job as of yet, but I thank God that I am not where I was. All this change happened at a time where I had to isolate and there was really nowhere to go. God kept me out of the hospital. I am alive and I believe that the best is yet to come!! God literally took everything and showed me all I need is Him; and I am better because of Him only. Hallelujah!!

Cleopatra Lewis

LIFE IS GOOD! THANK YOU JESUS

Even in the midst of a Pandemic God is Still God! I remember sitting one Sunday in the presence of God and the city of Boston was beginning to shut down due to the coronavirus. I was still working at the Medical Center, I heard The Spirit of the Lord say it's time for you to go, take a leave.

I wasn't feeling that great, my body was aching, I had headaches, I had stomach pains, along with a lot of things going on at work. Mentally, work was draining and I couldn't sleep at night, but in the mist of all of that God was good. I kept hearing the Spirit of the Lord say it's time for you to go. I remember going into work telling my boss I'm ready to take a leave of absence she said, I cannot let you go right now I have not heard anything from your union.

At that point God moved and the President of the Hospital sent out an email with how there was going to be furloughs throughout the hospital. We were offered packages and I took one. When I received my package in April I said Lord I trust you. I've been home for months now, and God has made a way to put food on my table, to have all my bills paid, and to be a blessing to others. We are all in this pandemic together.

I have learned that sharing is caring and kindness is very important. We have been given a gift called life and that we should appreciate it. In this pandemic I've discovered that God is still good and that He's healing and keeping his children.

I've also learned that we need each other. There is no rainbow without rain, and this too shall pass. Just know that better days are coming. Life is a lesson, and we need to be grateful to God for all of His many blessings towards us. Nobody but God can do these things.

Llewyen Dingle

REPAIRING DURING THE PANDEMIC

My home was one of the most unsightly looking houses in my neighborhood. Battered, withered and rotted wood panels encased the large front porch. The sight of my home was getting to a point of embarrassment.

Even worst, my upper porch was so frail I was afraid a strong wind storm would blow it to down! How could this be? I had a job, I had income, but I also had expenses and repairing my property did not fit into my budget.

One way to get from under this predicament was to downsize and sell; a thought which frequently crossed my mind. And then out of nowhere Covid19 hit the world stage! I lost my job the same week it was declared a pandemic. Here I am a single mother supporting a first year college student, caring for my grandfather, and hearing my tenant also lost her job. Now I had to face all of this with my main source of income gone! But fear not!!! I didn't let my faith fail me.

I remembered 10 years ago I was faced with almost the same predicament. Because of that experience I could rely on the very same God who brought me out back then to do it again! He's Able!!!

After the layoff, I collected unemployment with the extra federal funds from the Cares Act. To my surprise my job of 3 years gave me a severance package. My neighbors and local food pantries gave me more than enough food that I barely went to the grocery store. Covid19 closed college dorms which gave my child a refund balance instead of a balance due!

In this pandemic I have found myself with more funds than I have had in a long time. I paid my tithes, mortgage, and bills without interruption. In addition I was equipped financially to do what I've been yearning to do for quite a while- home repair. Seven months later after Covid19 first hit, I can testify my home is no longer the ugly duckling of the neighborhood. God has allowed me dwell in safety from Covid19 in the comfort of my better looking home.

Missionary Diane Norman

THE LORD IS MY SHEPHERD

My testimony is, in the midst of a pandemic- God continues to bless his people. Last year, I was faced unexpectedly with a large equipment repair; without having the available funds to fix or replace it. The task of repairing the central air unit in my out of state property, was a major challenge.

My tenants leasing the property for the year, became impatient with the process it took to properly fix the unit. The first repair call was an emergency fix. It got the unit working temporarily, until the system failed again. This repair method seemingly was unrealistic, very costly and not resolving the issue. At this point, replacing the unit was the best conclusion to achieve a permanent remedy. Three contractors, quoted me the cost to install a New Central Air Unit, from $3800-$7400. I tried to get financed through several contractors and lending agencies. Sadly, I kept getting denied. Unable to secure a loan and get the equipment replaced. The tenants decided to break their lease early and vacate the premises, because of No Central Air.

This financial setback hit me really hard. Especially now, with the unexpected loss of income and facing unpaid bills needing to be paid. I felt devastated, not knowing how I was going to recover from this heavy blow that hit me. All I could do was trust in God. "The Lord is my shepherd" (Psalm 23:1a, KJV), and "For I know the plans I have for you" (Jer. 29:11a, NIV). What I didn't realize was, he had already turned things around for my good.

In the midst of the COVID-19 pandemic; God chose to bless me financially and mentally. I was able to qualify for a Small

Business Association loan making it possible for me to purchase the new Central Air and Furnace combination replacing the broken unit. In addition, a great new family became my new tenants renting the property this year.

God's Love lifted me from being Challenged to being a Champion; and realizing there is a winner in me I'm more than a Conqueror, finances were stable again with rental and new tenancy. I am slowly regaining all which I lost in the year prior. Thank You Lord for All your Goodness and your Mercy towards me. Bless Your Holy Name.

Glenda Gaines-Meadows

No weapon that is formed against thee Shall prosper...

Isaiah 54:17a, KJV